MASTER THE ART OF CLOSING THE SALE

THE GAME-CHANGING 10-STEP SALES PROCESS FOR GETTING MORE CLIENTS AND REFERRALS

MASTER THE ART OF
CLOSING THE SALE

THE GAME-CHANGING 10-STEP SALES PROCESS FOR GETTING MORE CLIENTS AND REFERRALS

BENJAMIN BROWN

Master the Art of Closing the Sale
The Game Changing 10 Step Sales Process for Getting
More Clients and Referrals

Benjamin Brown

Published by: 360 Sales Consulting

www.360SalesConsulting.com

ISBN: 978-0692660058

Praise for Master the Art of Closing the Sale

"Ben has hit it out of the park! This book is very easy to read yet still powerful. It introduces ten essential steps to sell any product or service. I really liked real-life stories supporting each step. A smart investment for any salesperson."

Greg Gutkowski
Internet marketing strategist and bestselling author of 9 Best Kept Steps Of B2B Digital Marketing

"Ben Brown walks the WALK! His sales experience and practical knowledge are clearly displayed in this exceptional explanation and applicable description of the sales process. Ben also puts the 'fun' back in fundamental as he shows how even the most fearful person can succeed in sales with the proper mindset, tools, and techniques. This book will be in a prominent position on my bookshelf and I'll review it often."

Russ Barnes, Colonel (Ret. US Army)
Founder of Systro Consulting

"Ben Brown takes a holistic approach to touch on all major points essential in preparing the salesperson and a company's sales process for optimum success. Ben highlights the importance of training, rehearsal, and preparation in order to achieve and win the results while focusing on the prospect's needs and meeting them."

Rachid Zahidi
CEO of Sentinel Background Checks and bestselling author of *The Business Immunity System*

"This quick read highlights all of the important steps in a sales process to make them memorable. Even seasoned veterans forget the critical parts when they are in the mix, especially when qualifying a prospect and affirming that they are capable of buying what you are selling. I recommend this fresh take on sales no matter your level of experience."

Koby Brya
Founder of InnovativeFront and author of *#Integrity: Developing a Principled Life*

"What do consistently high-performing salespeople do? They follow Ben Brown's ten-step sales system. Thoughtful, focused, and comprehensive, the book will equip you with all the tools you need to build strong sales performance for yourself and your team. Ben's ten critical steps are rooted in a long career in sales and a deep understanding of human psychology. Learn how to eliminate frustration and time-wasting activities and how to turn leads into sales and sales into referrals."

Sanaa Belfekih, MBA
Marketing consultant and TV producer

"Ben Brown has distilled the essence of what it takes to be successful in sales into ten clear, precise steps. Great foundational info here for new salespeople, and experienced reps will discover new secrets for taking their business to the next level."

Howard VanEs
President, Let's Write Books, Inc.

"Need results? Selling is a more competitive game than ever. And preparation as well as being able to relate to a potential client are essential to successful sales. Master The Art of Closing will certainly give you or your team the proven skill sets to be able to close the deal and get more referrals. The strategies Ben Brown shares in this book are proven to work. I highly recommend it."

Chris Gibson
Bestselling author, entrepreneur, and lifestyle coach

Foreword

Having traveled across the globe delivering workshops and events to many cultures, personally coaching hundreds of professionals in many industries involving numerous products and services the one thing that is always a constant regardless of culture, industry, product or service, is that the laws governing the art of successful sales always directly apply.

What Ben Brown has illustrated so clearly and elegantly in this book is a sequential 10 step process that, if followed, will create an unstoppable flow of qualified prospects, clients and referral sources. This, after all, is the life-blood of every organization and its guarantee of future viability.

Whether you are a small business owner, sales manager or sales representative you must have a successful process to effectively and efficiently produce sales.

For over 30 years I have dedicated my life to the leadership development and public speaking quality of leaders in business, government and community. Whether it's motivating or inspiring their audiences, employees, voters, donors, customers or clients, the one common denominator that all highly successful leaders share is their ability to be or become really good salespeople.

Here are a few important suggestions for getting the most from Ben Brown's book:

1. **First, decide you want to positively influence more people, create more sales and see your business dramatically increase.**

2. **Understand that having a standard, workable process, such as the one in this book, makes for reliable results.**

3. **As you begin reading, reflect on how each of the 10 principles laid out in Ben's book personally applies to your sales process as well as your life.**

4. **Make a conscious decision to use these steps to build your prosperity and success.**

5. **Practice, practice, practice until you are effortlessly using these 10 steps so well, they are second nature.**

I have always coached in the direction of greatness. If you truly want to be a great professional at anything, you must motivate and inspire others to achieve way beyond their limits. This takes sales skill and you must exemplify greatness yourself.

Now read "Master the Art of Closing the Sale: The Game Changing 10 Step Sales Process for Getting More Clients and Referrals" and get ready to take your business to a whole new level.

Greatness awaits!

Joe Yazbeck,
President, CEO, Prestige Leadership Advisors
Author, Best-seller No Fear Speaking
International Speaker & Coach
www.nofearspeaking.com

Table of Contents

Introduction . . . .

The 360 Sales Process in Action . . . .

Step 1: Getting Prepared . . . .

Step 2: Research and Relate . . . .

Step 3: Qualify Potential Customers. . . . .

Step 4: Identify Emotional Triggers . . . .

Step 5: Set Up the Offer . . . .

Step 6: Present the Offer . . . .

Step 7: Close on Product Concepts. . . . .

Step 8: Close on Price and Terms . . . .

Step 9: Ask for Money . . . .

Step 10: Get Testimonials and Referrals . . . .

Conclusion. . . . .

Acknowledgements . . . .

Recommended Reading. . . . .

About the Author . . . .

Introduction

"...success leaves clues, and people who produce outstanding results do specific things to create those results."

–Tony Robbins

Chances are good that you are reading this book because you want to either improve your sales skills, are a sales manager looking for a solid training method, or you're a newbie who is just getting into sales and wants to learn to do it right. Well, congratulations, you have come to the right place!

I promise that reading this book will help you to:

- **Discover the secrets for turning skeptics into buyers and buyers into referral machines**

- **Learn how to stop wasting time with those who will never purchase from you and quickly identify those who will**

- **Use a proven step-by-step sales system that will skyrocket your success and give you rock solid confidence in selling**

- **Improve your communication skills and ability to influence others, both in business and in your personal life**

Before I explain more about what you'll find here, please indulge me for a moment as I tell you how I came to write this book and why you should listen to me.

Like Zig Zigler, Frank Bettger, Jeffrey Gitomer, and other sales greats, I love selling. It is in my heart and in my soul. I clearly remember my very first sales job twenty-two years ago selling health club memberships at Golds Gym; I really enjoyed working with people, helping them meet their fitness goals, and I was making more money than I had ever in my life. I couldn't have been more excited to be there and I was hooked on selling!

As I took on different positions over time selling cars, computer products and services, voice recognition software, staffing services, and transportation services, my skills grew. However, I wanted to be a super-successful salesperson, so I began experimenting with different tools and techniques to see what worked and what didn't. I also interviewed highly successful salespeople to gain an insight into their magic sauce. As I started to implement what I was learning, I began to dramatically improve my closing percentages as well as the number of referrals I was receiving.

Other salespeople and managers noticed what I was doing and asked that I teach my techniques to them; their sales grew exponentially as well. As much as I love selling, I also love training and teaching others, which led me to formalize my training model and start my company, 360 Sales Consulting.

In preparation for this book I interviewed top buyers—people who have the decision-making authority to purchase hundreds of thousands of dollars. If the sales process is a dance, it's important to know with whom one is dancing.

One of the buyers was a former IT director for a national supermarket chain. He told me about one of the larger computer companies who sent in a team of twelve people to try and sell their very expensive equipment. As he spoke, I realized even these huge organizations could use a better sales system. They started their sales process without even asking who had the authority to make a purchase. They didn't ask the right questions to figure out what kind of equipment the potential client needed. Apparently their approach was to overwhelm the prospect with fancy suits, big words, golf outing invitations, and shiny smiles. Some people call this the "Show Up and Throw Up" methodology—reminiscent of throwing mud at the wall to see what sticks.

The problem is that these salespeople do not have a good process in place, and without a good system they are just flailing around and hoping that someone notices and makes a purchase. Remarkable as it may be, many small to midsize companies simply do not have a systemized sales training program, yet sales is the life blood of any business!

I am genuinely excited to share the 360 Sales System with you, for as you embark on this journey, you will come to be in control of the sales cycle, have more fun, and enjoy greater income and confidence. Let's get started!

Bonus Offers:

Three FREE sales training videos

Daily planner to keep you on track every day!

Download them here:
www.360SalesConsulting.com

The 360 Sales Process in Action

"You don't need a big close, as many sales reps believe. You risk losing your customer when you save all the good stuff for the end. Keep the customer actively involved throughout your presentation, and watch your results improve."

– Harvey Mackay

L arry, a good friend of mine and the CEO of a major grocery chain, recently mentioned to me that he had just spent over $5,000 on a new computer. I was curious: Why on earth would anyone spend that much money on a computer when you can get them for under $500 these days? That must be a very special computer!

"Well, actually, I didn't go into the shop expecting to spend that much money," he explained. "But it was so perfect; I mean it was like the salesperson read my mind or something. She didn't pressure me, didn't try and make me buy anything, and it just became obvious that this was the computer for me."

I pressed him for more information. I mean, the guy was practically gushing about the experience he had with a salesperson. How often does that happen?

"Like I said," he continued, "I didn't plan on making such a big purchase that day. I knew I needed a good computer, better than average, so I called a friend and asked if he knew of someone who could get me a great deal. He told me about his purchasing experience with a woman named Sally, explaining that he got an incredible deal on an exceptional computer. He gave me her number and I made an appointment for that afternoon."

Okay, I thought to myself, Sally understood the power of testimonials and referrals, which is step ten of the 360 Sales Consulting process. She had done a good job on her last sale, and the word of mouth of her performance did a lot of her work for her. She did so well that she didn't even have to find the new client; he found her.

"Sally was waiting for me at her office, dressed very professionally, and she gave me a firm handshake," Larry told me. "She offered me coffee or water and made small talk for a few minutes. She put me at ease almost immediately, asking me a few questions about myself as we walked into her office next to the showroom. She had obviously done a little homework, which made the whole conversation much easier. When I made the appointment I had mentioned where I worked, and she had taken the time to check out the company web site as well as my own LinkedIn profile. I was amazed at how well she had prepared for my visit."

It looked like Sally had followed step one, Getting Prepared, before she arrived at work. She was mentally and physically prepared for the day. She was alert and ready to face her customers and make those sales.

Based upon Larry's comments, Sally had also done a great job with the second step of sales: Research and Relate. She had done her research before he arrived and used the information to immediately form a bond with him. When they met, she put him at ease right away with good eye contact, excellent attire, and appropriate small talk.

"Once we sat down we got right to business. Sally asked me if I intended to make the purchase today or if anyone else needed to be involved in making the decision. I assured her that since I am the CEO, this was my decision and I had the money in my budget. At that point I didn't expect to spend $5,000–not in my wildest dreams! I explained my problem. I had an older computer and it was incredibly slow. I needed something faster. Sally said she understood and we continued talking."

This is an excellent example of how to execute step three of sales: Qualify Potential Customers. We'll go into that in more detail later in this book, but the idea is to ensure that your prospect has a problem, is the decision maker, and can make the purchase today.

"I felt very comfortable with her and within minutes I was relating the story of how another executive just got a new, very expensive computer, and everyone was so envious. I was kind of jealous of the attention he was getting."

This is the point where you get down to the real reasons why the client wants to make a purchase. Sure, he needs a new computer, but what does he really want from that computer? In this case, my friend gave Sally his emotional trigger, or the reason why he wanted to buy. My friend had been putting up with a slow computer for a long time. However, what was really motivating his purchase was that he wanted to look good to his co-workers; he wanted to out-shine his other executives.

"Then, Sally asked me if she presented me with a computer that met all of needs, if I would be inclined to make the purchase today. I told her I would—only if it met all my needs, though."

That's step five of sales: Set Up for the Offer. Sally asked Larry if he was prepared to make the purchase if his problem was resolved. Once she received affirmation, she could continue with the process.

"At this point Sally invited me into the showroom and walked me right over to a sleek-looking computer with a big, crystal-clear screen. She spent a few minutes showing me some of the features and explained that this was the type of computer successful executives opted for. It was fast, beautiful, and practically oozed professionalism."

I'll get into this in detail in the chapter on step six: Present the Offer, but you can see how Sally had listened to what my friend really wanted—a computer that made him look like an executive—and showed him exactly that. She didn't get into the technical details, instead focusing on the features that resolved his needs and problems.

"Sally paused and asked me if this was what I wanted," my friend continued his explanation. "I was thrilled and by that point I had to have that computer. It was exactly what I wanted."

Sally received agreement from her prospect that the computer she presented was something he wanted and would purchase. This is step seven: Closing on Product Concepts.

"When Sally told me the price I almost fell over. I mean, $5,000, even for a high-end computer, seemed a bit excessive. But I looked at the computer and I knew I had to have it. Sure, it was a luxury, but I'm the CEO of a major company and an executive needs to look the part. So when Sally asked if I wanted that machine at that price, I agreed right away. What choice did I have?"

This was a great use of step eight: Close on Price and Terms. By this point, the CEO was definitely going to make that purchase, and Sally confirmed it. She's almost there.

"Next," my friend continued, "she asked if I was going to pay with a credit card or purchase order. I gave her my card and we rung up the sale right there."

Good job, Sally! She got the sale by completing step nine of sales: Ask for the Money. Many salespeople have trouble at this stage of the game. As I'll discuss in the chapter on step nine, you have to get over that fear and get their money.

"Then Sally did something I didn't expect," the CEO continued. "She asked for a testimonial and some referrals. I was so happy with my new computer that I was thrilled to give a glowing report, as well as three referrals. And, of course, I tell anyone who needs a new computer where they should go to get excellent service."

And that brings the sales process to a close. Sally got her testimonials and referrals, which is step ten of sales. These will lead her to more closed deals down the road.

Here is an overview of the ten steps Sally used. The rest of the book will go into depth about each one and show you how to implement them effectively.

1. **Get Prepared –** Every day there are tasks that all sales personnel must perform to be ready to meet the day. Spend some time each morning exercising both your body and mind, and organize your priorities so you get to work knowing what needs to be done first.

2. **Research and Relate –** You can dramatically improve your chances of making the sale if you research your prospect, even briefly, before meeting them. You can use this research, along with your body language,

dress, and conversation, to create a
comfortable space for your potential client.

3. **Qualify Potential Customers –** Find out who has
    the authority to make a decision. Determine that
    they have a problem that needs to be resolved
    and whether or not they have the money in
    their budget to purchase the product or service.
    It's important not to waste time and effort on
    individuals who do not have spending authority,
    a need for the product or money to purchase.

4. **Identify Emotional Triggers –** Next, you talk
    to your prospect and find out what emotional
    need they're trying to satisfy. By finding out
    how they want to feel, what would happen if
    the problem was not solved, and so forth, you
    can then explain to them, in the next step,
    how your product can meet those needs.

5. **Set up the Offer –** Ask your prospect if he
    or she would be willing to purchase an item
    (today) if it could solve his/her problems.
    This is where you find out if your prospect
    is serious about making a purchase.

6. **Present the Offer –** Now it's time to present
    to your potential customer. Don't make
    the mistake of doing a long, technical
    presentation. You are fulfilling the emotional
    triggers that you previously identified.

7. **Close on Product Concepts (Handle Objection)** – Lay out your solution to the problems of your customer, and get agreement that your solution is what is wanted. Handle any objections.

8. **Close on Price and Terms** – Now you get to the price and terms. Tell your prospect what it's going to cost and get their agreement. If there are objections, handle them here.

9. **Ask for Money** – After all the work you've done to get to this point, you must ask for payment. This is an essential step and by this time the new client should be happy to write you a check or pull out their credit card.

10. **Get Testimonials and Referrals** – As soon as you've received payment in one form or another you need to ask for referrals and a testimonial. You need to get this right away; life gets busy, and a client can't forget if they do this right away.

As you can see from Larry's experience and the outline above, each step builds on the previous one. Getting agreement at each phase is essential before moving on to the next step—we'll cover this in more detail as we go through book.

When sales are performed using these steps the process goes smoothly. Your days will become easier, your life more fun, and your income and statistics will improve. As you read this book you will learn these steps and when you become an expert at applying them, you will be closing deals fast and efficiently. That is how sales are supposed to work.

*"Sales is an art, when done right
it's a beautiful thing."*

– Ben Brown

Step 1:
Getting Prepared

*"Sales are contingent upon the attitude of the
salesman - not the attitude of the prospect."*

– W. Clement Stone

When you arrive at the office each day, do you feel refreshed and ready for anything the world throws at you? Are you completely prepared, having identified your priorities and goals? Do you feel relaxed and at ease? If you are like most people today, you rush out of the house without eating a good breakfast, don't exercise in the morning (or at all), almost never read a book, and rarely have time for any meditation or other spiritual practice. If that is you, you may agree with me that when you come to work, you aren't entirely ready to take on the world.

If you want to be a top-performing salesperson, you'd better start by ensuring you spend some time each morning preparing for the day ahead. It's amazing how big of a difference that time can make to your ability to connect with your clients and generate sales.

Take a look at my friend Jeff, for example. His sales were down and he didn't understand why. He was working hard—sixty hours a week or more—and using every trick he knew to close deals. Yet nothing seemed to work and now it was Monday, the beginning of another week of twelve-hour work days. He was tired, and as usual after a weekend, had to rush out the door within minutes after waking up, He barely had the time to drink a cup of coffee, which is an essential nutrient to many businesspeople.

Jeff arrived late to work and poured over his to-do list. He realized in a moment of panic that he had to be at a meeting with a prospect in a few minutes. At the meeting, he called the potential client by the wrong name and had trouble answering several questions about the product. He got flustered and the prospect ended the meeting earlier than Jeff had expected. A short time later, the potential client sent Jeff an email to let him know that he was not going to sign a contract with Jeff's company. Jeff realized that the client's decision was a reflection of the unsuccessful meeting.

Jeff realized he'd better do something quickly. His livelihood as well as his sanity and self-respect depended on it!

PREPARATION IS KEY

"By failing to prepare, you are preparing to fail."

– Benjamin Franklin

Regardless of your profession, whether you are in sales or something else entirely, you need to ensure that you are operating at peak efficiency. An excellent way to do this is to spend an hour each morning shaking off the cobwebs that built up overnight so you can orient yourself to the new day.

I call this the Power Hour. It's the time between when you roll out of bed and when you jump in the car to get to the office. This is the most important time of the day, since it sets the mood the moment you walk in the door at work. Ensuring you complete this daily routine can make the difference between failure and success.

Think about the person who jumps out of bed, quickly showers, and dashes off to the office a few minutes later, making a quick stop at the local coffee shop for a danish and a latte. By the time this person gets to the office, he or she hasn't even woken up yet and is not even close to being ready to face the day and make some sales. The only reason they can function at all is because of the caffeine and sugar gulped before arriving.

This is not a good way to succeed in any profession, much less sales. Anyone who operates in this manner for any length of time is going to have problems. Let's say this person gets to work at nine in the morning. This means that their first hour in the office, assuming they are not stuck in a meeting, is spent reading emails and trying to figure out their priorities for the day.

Working in this way is not only bad for your professional life, but it can also harm your health. You will be more vulnerable to stress-related issues and diseases, and your mental and emotional well-being will be reduced. In fact, anyone who consistently begins their day in this manner will start to hate their job as they will always be playing catch-up.

Wouldn't it be better to come into work feeling refreshed, powerful, and ready to begin? Don't you think you'll be more likely to land those sales if your mind is clear, your body is feeling good, and you've prioritized your tasks? Read on to find out how to start your day off right and be able to confront anything and anyone that comes your way.

PHYSICALLY

"An early-morning walk is a blessing for the whole day."

– Henry David Thoreau

Another salesperson, Jane, related to me how she had been one of the top salespeople at her company. Her statistics were always breaking new records, her job satisfaction was high, and her income seemed assured for the long term. But, that all changed a few years later. Every day seemed to drag and each sale was like pulling teeth. She hated her job, her morale was low, and she was dissatisfied with everything going on in her life.

What had altered to cause such a dramatic difference in her attitude and profession? Jane confessed to me that over the years, as she become busier and busier, she stopped doing her morning exercise routine. At first this seemed like a good idea. She had been going to the gym every morning for thirty minutes before heading into the office, but there was always more work to be done, so she figured she would gain back some time by sleeping in a bit later and skipping the gym.

Our bodies need exercise. It's as simple as that. Without a regular physical routine we tend to get sluggish and achy. It might seem that skipping thirty minutes on the exercise bike to get some extra sleep is a good idea, but the reality is quite different.

To start your sales day off right, you need to do some physical activity. It doesn't really matter what exercise you perform. Some people like to go to the gym every morning, others take a long walk, and some utilize a stationary bike or practice yoga. Whatever you choose, just make sure you do it as part of that first hour each day.

Once Jane started going to the gym each morning again, she found her energy returning and her days began to get smoother. She felt better as she worked and thus was able to focus on her sales and her clients and close more deals.

MENTALLY AND SPIRITUALLY

"Champions do not become champions when they win the event, but in the hours, weeks, months and years they spend preparing for it.

The victorious performance itself is merely the demonstration of their championship character."

– Alan Armstrong

The reasons behind Bob's slump in sales were a bit harder to pin down. During our discussion, Bob told me how sales had been his passion for much of his early life. He rocketed up to become the top salesperson at his company and received several large bonuses for his efforts. Yet somehow it all seemed empty, and even though he was making quite a bit of money, he didn't seem to care. There simply wasn't anything about life that excited him anymore.

Bob told me he always started his day with a good breakfast and thirty minutes of exercise at the local gym. After finishing his routine, he drove to the office to start his workday. The sales routine always went smoothly, but he found that he was having difficulties listening to his potential clients. He just didn't care anymore.

In addition to the body, it is also necessary to exercise the mind and spirit. In a busy world where everything needs to be done immediately and life moves very quickly, it is easy to neglect your mental and spiritual needs.

It is important to keep reading throughout life. Good books and articles refresh and relax the mind. Reading is how we gain new knowledge, how we share in the thoughts and lives of others, and how we relax. Even a few minutes with a good novel, magazine, or newspaper each morning can rejuvenate your mind and allow you to focus better throughout the day.

For those who believe in a spiritual side of life, spending a little time each morning mediating, praying, or doing whatever practice(s) are appropriate can be rejuvenating and invigorating. This makes it easier to face the problems and trials of the day–to confront prospects and to close those sales.

After Bob finished his sales training with us, he realized that he needed to exercise his mind and spirit each day. He adjusted his schedule so that he had some time to read a good novel; just twenty minutes each morning. In addition, he meditated briefly after his physical workout. By making these simple changes to his morning routine, Bob found his love and passion for his job and his affinity for his clients returning, and he couldn't wait to begin each new day.

GOAL SETTING AND PRIORITIZATION

"Setting goals is the first step in turning the invisible into the visible."

– Tony Robbins

During one of our 360 Sales Consulting seminars, a sales manager explained in frustration that his sales staff didn't seem to be operating at peak efficiency. By all appearances they were working very hard. In fact, most of them were putting in twelve to fourteen hours each day. Yet, for all their efforts, it didn't seem like they were getting that much done. Everyone was making sales, but the larger deals seemed to drag on forever and the prospects often gave up in frustration.

One of the most important parts of your morning routine should be deciding what you want to accomplish during the day. Many salespeople wait until they get into the office to set their goals and prioritize their tasks. The problem with this is that quite often the work starts immediately after you walk in the door. As a result, the average salesperson doesn't find the time to prioritize on a regular basis and almost never sets goals for each day.

Knowing your priorities and goals can be of great benefit; it can help you eliminate meetings that are not needed, figure out which phone calls can be skipped, and avoid spending time on paperwork that doesn't need to be done.

Every day there may be hundreds of tasks that need attention, and it is generally impossible to get through them all. Setting priorities before going to work lets you focus on those sales calls or other tasks that are most urgent or important. This also helps discard those tasks that do not need to be done (at least not now) along with potential clients who can wait.

Once the sales manager understood the importance of setting goals and priorities, he made it *his* priority to ensure each and every member of his staff was trained on this process. It didn't take long before their sales statistics rose higher than ever.

PRACTICE

"Tomorrow's victory is today's practice."

– Chris Bradford, *The Way of the Warrior*

As I mentioned, some of my research for this book included interviewing buyers as well as salespeople. One of these buyers mentioned to me that they had an experience with a salesperson named Doyle. They were not impressed with his sales presentation. He didn't seem to communicate very well, ignored their questions, and didn't acknowledge their comments. He appeared nervous, causing the buyer to believe he was not telling them the whole truth about the product.

By the time you have a prospect in front of you or on the phone, it is vital that you appear confident, knowledgeable, and comfortable. Sometimes even a slight hesitation or a failure to answer a question can doom a sale before it gets going.

You can improve your sales abilities by practicing scenarios over and over. The more you drill various scenarios, the better you will be able to sell. Drilling improves your ability to communicate with your prospects in a variety of situations.

Isn't it interesting that a football team spends forty hours or more each week getting ready for a sixty-minute game each weekend? All week long, the team drills the same plays over and over and practices until they can do it all perfectly. They do this for hours on end to prepare for those few minutes each weekend.

You can drill in a number of ways. One method is to video your sales pitch and watch the tape. You'll be surprised to find out how you sound and how your potential clients perceive you.

An even better method is to team up two salespeople to drill each other. One plays the client and the other the salesperson and they switch back and forth. They can practice any number of scenarios on each other, from handling objections to asking for the money. This allows any rough points to be drilled out in advance of seeing any prospects. You can also do this with a group of salespeople in a type of question-and-answer approach.

PRODUCT KNOWLEDGE

"Knowledge is power."

–Sir Francis Bacon

The purchasing director of a major supermarket chain detailed how he drove over sixty miles through traffic into downtown Los Angeles to meet with a salesperson about new refrigeration systems. He was ready to spend over a million dollars right then and there, assuming the product met his requirements.

The meeting got off to a good start. He met David, the lead sales manager; they shook hands and walked into the conference room together. The director was very happy with David's confidence and attire. This looked like it was going to be an easy fit for his needs.

Everything went wonderfully until the purchasing director began asking about the details of the product. The director needed to determine if the system would fit in each of his stores. David didn't know how big the refrigerators were, but he said he'd find out. Next the director wanted to know why he should buy David's product instead of the competitor's version. When David hesitated, the director, somewhat annoyed, told David to call him back when he finished his research. Unfortunately, by the time David got back to him, the deal was lost; the director had already purchased from another vendor.

It's embarrassing when a prospect asks about a product you are selling and you don't have an answer for them. Of course, there are occasions when you won't know highly technical details, but you'd better know the basics.

Make sure promotional materials about your product or service are available. If the product is technical, such as computer equipment, you might also have a few technical brochures ready or one of your technical experts available to answer more detailed questions.

The purchasing director went on to tell me about a purchase of trash compactors. He was very impressed with one of his vendors during the meetings about this very large sale. He asked a few technical questions, such as the exact dimensions and cooling requirements, which naturally the salesperson couldn't answer. Instead of hesitating or saying she'd get back to him, the salesperson immediately called a specialist, put him on speaker phone, and got those questions answered right away. A multi-million dollar contract was soon awarded as a result.

The prospect is likely to ask questions about your product or service. It would be an excellent idea to drill your knowledge over and over again. If possible, set aside time to have a sales associate quiz you on the details before a big meeting. Drill out those uncertainties.

A GOOD DAY SELLING

Jeff rolled out of bed at six and began his morning routine. He ate a good breakfast and spent thirty minutes on his exercise bike. Next, he went over the day in his mind, thinking of all of the tasks he knew he had to complete. As he thought, he wrote down the three most important ones that he would get to before anything else.

He set a goal of closing three sales, drilling his scripts and answers to questions with a fellow salesperson, and completing an online sales training course with 360 Sales Consulting. Jeff wrote those goals down on a piece of paper, which he would reference several times as he worked.

Finally, he spent a few minutes meditating, watered his plants, and drove to the office refreshed and ready to start his workday. He felt good knowing exactly what he needed to achieve and he gave a hearty greeting to the receptionist as she handed him his messages and listed his appointments for the day.

All three of his most important sales presentations scheduled for the morning were completed quickly, easily, and without problems. Jeff closed all of them, and even had time to close a forth one that came in unexpectedly after lunch. He completed his course, feeling very confident about the techniques he had learned, and spent an hour drilling as he had planned. By the end of the day, he was ready to go home. As always he felt refreshed, invigorated and full of energy.

For a FREE daily planning guide visit www.360SalesConsulting.com

Step 2:
Research and Relate

80% of sales require 5 follow-up calls after the meeting.[1] 44% of salespeople give up after 1 follow-up.[2]

During the first few moments of your initial meeting you have an opportunity to show your future clients that you care about them. You'll get off to a good start if you spend a few minutes in advance researching them and their company. This allows you to jump right into a conversation with them about their goals and what problems they are trying to solve instead of wasting time trying to figure out who they are and what they do.

In order to make a sale, you have to connect with the prospect and get them to relax and trust you. In a sales situation many people are distrustful, sometimes with good

---

1   http://blog.hubspot.com/sales/sales-statistics
2   http://blog.hubspot.com/sales/sales-statistics

reason, and feel stressed and tense. Your mission during this step is to get them to relax so they will listen to your message and be willing to continue forward towards the sale. By looking professional and understanding your client, you should be able to achieve that result.

RESEARCHING THE POTENTIAL CLIENT

"The toughest thing about the power of trust is that it's very difficult to build and very easy to destroy. The essence of trust building is to emphasize the similarities between you and the customer."

– Thomas J. Watson

Sally attended one of the 360 Sales Consulting seminars because she was new to sales and needed to learn the basics. She told me that she had been surprised a few days earlier when her supervisor called and asked her to meet with some new potential clients because her supervisor was ill and couldn't make it. Regardless, the meeting had to proceed so the sale could be made. This put Sally into a panic. She didn't know anything about these people!

The meeting between Sally and the prospect didn't go well at all. Sally understood the product very well, but she and the future client just couldn't seem to get on the same page. They never relaxed enough to want to sit down and listen. Sally could see there was no connection, and even though she was new to the game, she understood that without this, there would be no sale.

Before your prospects arrive, it is a good idea to do some research to find out more about them. An excellent way to impress them during the first meeting is to show that you understand their point of view and you share some common ground.

If you have your potential client's business card or a brochure then you should have their name, the name of their company, and most likely their web site address.

- **Review their company web site quickly to find out what products or services they produce or sell. A lot of sites have a "History of the Company" or an "About" section; these can be very useful in your research to give you a little more understanding of their corporate culture and beliefs. Find out how long the company has been in business and get details on any mergers or acquisitions.**

- **Look at your prospect's Facebook profile. You'll only get to see what they have posted as public but often there is some interesting data there. People sometimes post about their hobbies or places they have traveled.**

- **Check out their LinkedIn and Twitter profile. This will give you a lot of information about your prospect. What company do they work for? What school(s) did they attend? Who were their previous employers?**

- **If you discover that your prospect has a blog, a vlog (video blog), or a web site then you can truly find out an immense amount of data about them.**

- **Sometimes you may find their photographs on the web. A quick look through their pictures can give you a lot of information.**

It is tempting to spend a long time doing this research. Remember though, your purpose is to create a bond with your prospective clients, not find out about their entire lives. A quick analysis using these tools will help you understand more about them and enable you to put them at ease so they are willing to open up and communicate.

Avoid the temptation to immediately overwhelm your prospect with all of your newfound knowledge. Instead, just use the data that you've learned to work bits into a conversation. Your goal is create a comradery with your prospect. Volunteering too much about him or her can make them feel awkward and push them away, which is the opposite of what you want.

If they do start to feel uncomfortable with the amount of knowledge you have about them, it is best to confess that you did a few minutes of research. Usually this will put them at ease right away.

A few days later, Sally's supervisor needed her to take over another appointment as he was running late and client was early. Having learned from her mistake last time, she asked the receptionist to invite the prospect into the conference room and delay them a bit by offering coffee. She knew exactly what she needed to do.

With only a few minutes available, Sally jumped on the Internet and quickly performed some basic research using LinkedIn, Facebook, and Google. Within ten minutes, all the time she could get away with, she felt she knew enough about the prospect to be able to have a decent conversation with him. In fact, she was amazed to find that learning a few facts calmed her nerves and allowed her to be more relaxed and confident during that meeting.

RELATING TO THE PROSPECT

"First impressions matter. Experts say we size up new people in somewhere between 30 seconds and two minutes."

– Elliott Abrams

There are many ways to get the conversation going. For example, you could talk about their recent merger, mention something about their CEO, or ask about an award they won. The point is to find something to break the ice and get them talking and comfortable.

You want your future client to be calm and relaxed so you can ask questions without the meeting seeming like a hard sales pitch. Your purpose is to work with them to find a problem you can solve with your goods or services. You want them to feel like you care and want to help, and the best way to do that is to really care and truly want to help.

Dave is the vice president at Jarred Motors, and he had just driven an hour in heavy traffic to get to a sales meeting to discuss purchasing direct mail advertising services. He was impressed when Fred greeted him at the door, dressed smartly in a business suit, and gave him a firm handshake. Dave immediately felt at ease as Fred walked him to the conference room, asked if he wanted coffee or water, and questioned him about his company's recent merger.

The two of them spoke for a few minutes before the conversation naturally moved to business. Dave was so happy with the way things were going that he barely noticed that the focus had changed. After thirty minutes Fred asked if Dave was okay with proceeding forward, and Dave agreed without even thinking about it. Of course he was going to do business with Fred; he and his company were top-notch and professional.

Now that's a sale that is certainly going to close on a good note!

To get more tips on how to "Research and Relate" visit the 360 Sales Consulting web site.

Step 3: Qualify Potential Customers

"Qualifying your sales lead is the first and most important step in getting new business you'll be able to retain."

– Blake Lawrence, founder and CEO, Hurdat/Opendorse, Lincoln, Neb.

Have you ever spent hours, or even days, working on a sale only to find out you have been speaking with the wrong person? What about those times you were sure you had the deal ready to close only to learn that your potential customer didn't have enough money to purchase or didn't have a use for the product? I understand your frustration.

I remember a time, early in my sales career, when I flew all the way across the country to work with a prospect. That was an almost six-hour flight, on my own dime, for what I believed was going to be a major sale. I'm sure you know that feeling of excitement that comes with the anticipation of landing a big one.

I decided to allow the whole day, booked a room at a local hotel, and proceeded to the prospect's office by mid-morning. We met, shook hands, and then headed out for lunch at a very expensive restaurant. After lunch, the potential client and I headed back to his office and spent several hours in deep discussions about our products and services. Everything was going exceptionally well. The future customer was very interested in what we had to offer and was very attentive throughout the entire presentation. I knew the answers to all his questions and handled every single objection he came up with.

I'm sure you've figured out what's coming next. When I asked the prospect for a purchase order the room got silent. The only sound for several seconds was the gentle rush of air from the ventilation system.

"Well," my future customer began after that long pause. "I'm really sorry, but I don't have the authority to make this kind of decision, and I'm not sure we have the money in our budget for this type of purchase."

My heart sank and I mentally kicked myself. I had forgotten the third step of sales: Qualify the Potential Customer.

WHY THE THIRD STEP IS IMPORTANT

Wouldn't it be great to be able to eliminate the time wasted going after sales that never seem to pan out? Don't you think it would be useful to spend just a few minutes with each prospect to learn if a sale is possible instead of investing countless hours on one that is not going to happen?

This is the biggest time-saving step out of all the rules. I'm sure you can recall many instances when you, or someone you know, finished a full presentation about your product and its benefits only to find out that you were speaking to the wrong person.

This is very demotivating and has a number of effects on the sales representatives:

1. **The time spent pitching the product or service is lost forever.**

2. **The money and effort spent to find your prospect is wasted.**

3. **Questions may linger in the sales representative's mind as to why they didn't get the sale.**

MAKE SURE YOU'RE SPEAKING TO THE RIGHT PERSON

As soon as you've connected with the prospect it's absolutely essential that you determine whether or not they have the authority to make a purchasing decision. If you don't clarify this point right away, odds are that you are completely wasting your time.

Sometimes the prospect simply doesn't have the authority to make a decision. This could be an employee who has been asked to do some research or a manager who must get his boss' approval. In each of these cases you are wasting your time with them.

Let's look at another example. A salesperson at a major electronics chain begins the sales process with Ted, who has shown interest in purchasing a new computer. The salesperson shows off the various models and their features and prices, spending over an hour with Ted and ignoring other customers.

Finally Ted indicates that he has found the computer that he wants and the salesperson asks him how he wants to pay for it. At this point Ted mentions he has to go talk to his wife about it. The salesperson mentally kicks himself, knowing that he's probably lost the sale.

In fact, he never had a chance to make the sale in the first place. Chances are Ted will go home and try and convince his wife to let him purchase the new computer. His wife may not agree, and that's the end of that sale. It's also possible his wife may agree to the purchase but from a different place.

How do you find out if the prospect has the authority to make a purchase? One method is to ask them directly. If the direct approach seems a bit daunting, you can also ask leading questions to find out who else needs to be involved in the purchase. For example: "If you were going purchase these computers for your staff, is there anyone else who would be involved in the final decision?" or "Is there anyone else who would benefit by being a part of our presentation today?" This is an excellent subject to drill with other salespeople as discussed in the "Getting Prepared" section.

FIND OUT IF THEY HAVE A PROBLEM TO BE SOLVED

"Sales is all about solving a real problem for my clients. If I can help them to identify the problem and assemble the right solution, then 'the sale' is just a natural outcome."

– Clint Carlos, chief fun officer, GearFiveStudio, Lincoln, Neb.

My friend, the IT director of a major supermarket chain, related a story about the day a couple of salespeople stopped by his office. They bought lunch for him at an expensive restaurant and spent the better part of two hours talking about their new product. After they returned to his office, the conversation continued, complete with a slide presentation.

After the presentation, the director wanted to know why they were there. He had no use for their product and he didn't understand why they had spent so much time going over products that he was not going to purchase.

The salespeople had violated one of the components of the third step of sales—they didn't find out if the client had a problem that they could solve with their products and services. Instead of doing the basic footwork to find out that answer, they just "pitched and wished," hoping they could stumble across a sale. They should have saved everyone's time by asking a few simple questions up front.

Before you get very far into the sales process you need to find out if the prospect has a real problem that you can solve. Don't assume that you already know the answer or that everyone will want your product. Whenever you make this kind of assumption you waste time and energy.

You need to ask the right questions to confirm there is something to be solved. Additionally, if the problem is not profound or pressing then they will not be 100% committed to pursuing a solution.

Some useful questions include:

1. **Do you think that you have a problem?**

2. **How long have you been dealing with your issue?**

3. **How long have you been looking for a solution to your situation?**

4. **What products have you looked at before to help solve your problem?**

5. **What other products or services have you used to try and fix your problem?**

6. **Sometimes you have to create or point out the need. For example: If we can save you time and money over the product you are currently using would that be of interest to you?**

As the conversation proceeds and you get answers to these questions, you will get a feel as to whether the prospect has a legitimate challenge that your product or service can resolve and is interested in moving forward.

ENSURE THEY HAVE THE MONEY

Don't you think it would be important to find out if the customer has the money in his or her budget before you get too far along in the remaining sales steps? It's very disheartening to spend time trying to close the deal only to find out at the end that the money was not available in the first place.

Sometimes it's as simple as asking if they have the funds available on their credit card or in their checking account, while other times it's more complicated. You might have to deal with budgeting issues or spending limits, for example.

Some questions you can ask include:

1. **Do you want to solve this issue today?**

2. **Do you have the money in your budget to resolve this challenge?**

Remember though, you don't have to get down to the exact pricing of your products. All you want to do is get a general idea that the client not only is willing to solve his or her problem, but also has the money available to do so.

Knowing this information up front will save you a lot of time and energy, which you can utilize for those prospects who do have the ability to pay.

Once you have determined that the prospect has the authority to make a decision, has a problem to be resolved, and has the money, be sure to get approval to continue the sales process. This helps build a yes pattern and increases their desire to continue forward towards the close.

Step 4:
Identify Emotional Triggers

"There is one powerful distinction in sales that gives certain professionals a profound advantage: Regardless of what you are selling, whether its products, services, or advice, people buy based on feelings. They decide to buy when they experience certain feelings about a product or service AND the person offering it."

– Larry Pincu and Phil Glosserman, *Sell the Feeling*

I'd like to illustrate how emotional triggers help with sales by contrasting the approach of two salespeople. One person, Joe, uses the normal "pitch and wish" sales technique, while the other person, Jane, understands the emotional reasons people purchase and uses that information to close the sale.

The day had not gone well so far. It was almost lunchtime and Joe had not been able to sell a single car. He'd been approached by over a dozen customers and sometimes it seemed like they were interested, but no one purchased.

Joe was just about ready to head out to lunch when a young couple approached him and inquired about purchasing a new car. Joe smiled and walked them around the lot, showing them various models and reciting the advantages of each one. He steered the couple towards his personal favorite, a sporty two-door sedan, but they didn't seem interested. Joe shrugged to himself, kept smiling, and showed them car after car, explaining the advantages and disadvantages of each model on the lot.

Once in a while the couple showed some interest in one of the cars, but nothing seemed to gain their attention for very long. After they spent an hour looking at over twenty cars, the couple left without making a purchase. Joe took a late lunch, feeling a bit dejected and unhappy, not understanding why the couple didn't make a purchase. They seemed interested, and they had a problem to resolve— their old car needed to be replaced—but none of Joe's suggestions made them want to purchase.

On the other side of the car dealership, Jane met another couple as they walked onto the lot. She greeted them with a firm handshake and walked them into the lobby. She offered coffee, which they accepted, and talked with them for a few minutes. During this conversation, she quickly determined that the couple was tired of their old car because it was constantly breaking down. She also learned the two could make the decision, they were ready to buy today, and their credit was reasonably good.

Jane continued the conversation, keeping it light, and asked them more about their dream car. At first the couple appeared to agree they wanted something larger for their children, but within a few minutes Jane could see a hint of disagreement. She decided to question a bit further and discovered the husband wanted something sporty and his wife would prefer something roomy enough for the children.

With some further discussion, and a quick consultation with the finance manager, Jane worked out a plan for the couple to get two cars: a sporty car for him and a larger vehicle for her. With some creative financing, Jane created a deal where the price of two used cars was not that much more expensive than purchasing one new car. She worked the couple through the remainder of the sales process, closed the deal, and signed them on the bottom line.

THE REASONS WE BUY

Why do people buy? How do you sell something to someone? Many salespeople struggle because they use the "pitch and wish," meaning they are just throwing out ideas and words and hoping something captures the interest of the customer so they make a sale.

Take the example of purchasing a new car, for instance. When you stop and think about it, a car is transportation. It is a metal or fiberglass box on wheels designed to get one or more people from one point to another. Yet there are thousands of models, hundreds of shapes, and dozens of sizes. If a car is just for transportation, then why is there a need for so much variety?

There are so many models, shapes, and sizes because people have different emotional and stylistic needs that they want fulfilled. Some just want simple transportation, some need room for their kids, others need something "manly," some want speed, and others want to impress.

Science has proven in many cases people purchase because they have an emotional need, known as an emotional trigger, which the sale has fulfilled. This could be anything that the prospect sees as valuable beyond the specific problem that needs to be fulfilled.

These emotional triggers can be anything. For example, people respond to emotions such as greed or fear. They might want to appear more masculine or earn points with the boss or their spouse. Sometimes your prospect wants others to believe they have money and other times they want to give the impression that they are poor. A good salesperson asks questions that zero in on these emotional needs and then selects products or services that fulfill them.

For example, look at the way people buy technology. Whenever a new Apple product is released the masses start lining up days in advance to make sure they get the newest and greatest model. Similarly, thousands of people typically sign up to test new versions of Microsoft products just so they can say that they were among the first to have the experience.

Why do you suppose many people purchase a new smart phone every year or as soon as the newer, supposedly better model comes out? Sure, the new models have some extra features and a few new bells and whistles, but does anyone really need to change their phone so often?

These products are purchased because one or more emotional needs are fulfilled by the purchase. Take, for example, dishwashing liquid soap. Can you imagine a more boring product? Yet there are shelves of different soaps at the supermarket, in all colors, with different fragrances, different labels, and differently shaped bottles. Each of these fulfills a different emotional need.

Some folks might want to feel like they are helping the environment and purchase the "green" (supposedly better for the planet) dishwashing soap. Others are concerned about fragrances, so they purchase the soap that is fragrance-free. And probably some people want their liquid soap to match the colors in their kitchen.

Each of these is an emotional need that the customer fulfills when they buy the product. Sometimes the need is as simple as needing to be one of the first people to own a new thing. There are even a few people who need to be able to say they were THE first person to buy a product. At this stage of the sales process, your job is to talk to your prospect and figure out a need that your product or service can fulfill.

QUESTIONS TO ASK

Many times, sales representatives do not take advantage of the fourth step of sales because it requires asking some tough questions. Usually, you need to sit down with your prospects and get them to relax and open up about their motivations and personal choices. You can also talk to them about their personal life, their family and friends, their job, and anything else that comes up in the conversation.

Most prospects have not thought about their emotional triggers. These emotions generally fall below the conscious level. Thus, simply asking them directly will probably not be successful. This is why having a good conversation with your prospects is needed. You have to work out their needs and triggers yourself.

Once you have an understanding of those needs (negative or positive) you can make it relevant to the prospect. This lets you offer them the precise product or service to fulfill their emotional requirement.

Of course, you need to keep the conversation casual and beware of pushing too hard or too fast. You may ask a question which is too personal for your prospect, in which case you will need to back off a bit and try to get your answers from a different angle.

Some people will open up right away and tell you their whole life story. In this case, you may need to use the subtle art of interrupting or gently guiding the conversation to subjects more useful to your immediate goal.

You will find others who have built a seemingly impenetrable wall around themselves. Getting information from these people can be very tricky, but with skill you will be successful.

There are many questions you can ask in order to find out their emotional triggers. Some of these include the following.

1. **What would happen if you get your problem solved?**

2. **How would you feel?**

3. **How would you feel if you don't get your problem solved?**

4. **How would your day be different if you get your problem solved?**

5. **How would other people feel?**

For example, suppose you are selling a cleaning service, which offers to clean up an entire apartment in a single day. You have a prospect sitting in front of you and have established they have a problem they need to solve. Their apartment looks like a disaster area and they need it cleaned.

Once you start talking to them, you may ask questions such as:

- **How long has it been since the last cleaning?**

- **What will you do with the time you save?**

- **How does that make you feel?**

With the answers to these questions you can begin to build up a mental picture of why this potential client is asking for your service and what need they are trying to fulfill. This will help you find the correct product or service and close the sale.

While speaking with the prospect who needs cleaning products and services you might discover they have a bad back and thus cannot get on their hands and knees to scrub the floors. You could sell your service for health reasons since the prospect will have clean floors without hurting their back.

Perhaps the client may volunteer that they have people coming over and want to impress them. Thus, the deluxe cleaning service might be appropriate. With this information, not only did you find their emotional trigger, but you can now sell them the precise service required to fulfill that need.

If you have truly found the emotional trigger, then you will get a reaction from the prospect. This can be a facial expression, a change in their tone of voice, or a pause in the conversation. Once you see a reaction of that sort you can be confident that you've found the trigger you need. Be sure to get their approval to continue with the process, as you do for all the steps.

The purpose of step four is to create an emotional attachment as to why they want their problem solved. It is essential for you to understand the real reason your product will help them as this will give you both the information and confidence to close the sale.

Step 5: Set Up the Offer

*"Know what your customers want most
and what your company does best.
Focus on where those two meet."*

– Kevin Stirtz

Don't you think it would be a good idea to find out if your prospect is interested in solving his or her problem *before* you get any further into the sales process? Most salespeople make the mistake of assuming they can just proceed straight through the whole procedure. They want to get to the part where they ask for the money.

Before you even get to the offer you need to find out if your prospect wants to solve their problem. It's a simple fact that you cannot sell to someone who doesn't want his or her problem solved. So, by asking, you can save yourself time and heartache.

A colleague of mine, James, shared an incident where he didn't perform step five of the Steps of Sales, while calling on an IT director of a major retail chain. James said that was one of the worst mistakes of his career, and it affected the careers of several other people as well.

The IT director shared that they needed to move all of the computers in their IT department to Texas to protect them from the chance of being damaged in an earthquake. This was a huge project—a couple million dollars. The sales team knew it was going to be a tough sell to the CEO so they were careful to complete all of the previous steps.

The CEO was definitely the decision maker; the sales team had identified a problem, he agreed that it was a concern, and we knew the money was available. James knew they needed to find a solution to a serious problem in the event that they had an earthquake so they went ahead and hired some contractors to put together a proposal. In this case, preparing for the presentation to the CEO required quite a bit of work.

They engaged the services of two contractors and were all convinced they were working on a project that was sure to be approved. The contractors spent over 25 hours at no charge, assuming the project would be approved. They created drawings, wrote documents, and helped put an incredible plan together. James' staff put in numerous hours on the project as well.

Upon presenting the solution to the CEO he didn't even let the team continue. He said he was completely uninterested in the project because it wasn't a big enough problem that needed solving. He said he would never even think about approving it and wanted to know why the team had wasted so many resources putting it together.

James was personally devastated, as was his entire team. One of the contractors, the head of the project from her company, was demoted (they spent that much effort on it without charge) and she eventually left the company.

And all of that happened because they never asked the CEO if he *wanted* them to present (or in this case, do what was needed to set up for) the offer. If they had just done the simple step before they went to all the trouble of putting together an offer, they would have learned that the CEO didn't want us to solve his problem.

As I said before, many salespeople skip this step, going right past it to present the solution (a product or service.) This is one way that salespeople burn out quickly: they keep taking losses because they spend an inordinate amount of time on hopeless attempts to get sales when the prospect has no intention of solving their problem and thus purchasing your product or service. So why waste time going any further with them?

After learning about your potential client's issues, it is very possible that your product can help. At this time you need to find out if the customer is motivated enough to make the purchase. You do that simply by asking, "If I could solve that for you, are you willing to do business."

You might also want to add the word "today". Can we do business today? The reason being is that if the client wants to solve that problem and they cannot do it today they have to tell you why. This will help you uncover the issues you may need to address in your presentation so it doesn't come up in the close.

This is a very simple step. Don't make the mistake of overcomplicating it or trying to be clever. All you need to do is find out if your prospect wants the problem solved.

If you get agreement, then proceed to the next step. If not, then you're done. Move on to get contracts from people who actually want their problem resolved. That is all there is to it.

Step 6:
Present the Offer

Great leaders are almost always great simplifiers,
who can cut through argument, debate and doubt,
to offer a solution everybody can understand."

– Colin Powell

I'll bet you think this is the time to give your prospect a nice, full-feature presentation of what your product or service does and how it works. That would be a mistake. Instead, now that you've got permission from the prospect to continue with the sales process, it is time to present your emotionally satisfying solution to their problem. Focus on the problem and the emotional trigger and avoid the temptation to give a full presentation of all the features.

The purpose of the presentation is to build a yes pattern and promote buying signals.

Many salespeople lose the sale because their presentation is too long. I have many sales reps and entrepreneurs asking, "How long should my presentation be?" I tell them it should be long enough to cover the needs your clients has, get a yes pattern going, and listen for buying signals.

Ron, a salesperson for a major candy distributor, explained to me this recent experience with this step. He was very enthusiastic about his use of the rules of sales and how simple it was for him to close those deals now that he understood how it all works.

"Everything went perfectly," Ron told me during an interview for this book. "I was feeling fantastic, having made sure I was properly prepared for the day. I had an appointment with George, who is the candy purchaser for a chain of about twenty small stores.

I took the time to check him and his company out by looking at their web site and his LinkedIn profile. By the time he arrived I felt I was pretty well briefed, and I understood that the chain was small but doing very well. I was very confident that we had some products that would be of interest.

My receptionist greeted George when he arrived and seated him in the conference room. We shook hands and chatted for a few minutes, and I quickly learned that George wanted to improve the impulse candy sales for their stores. By impulse buys George meant the shelves next to the cash registers, which were supposed to be stocked with high-profit, fast-selling items. I also learned he was authorized to make the decision and the money was already approved.

As I probed further, George told me his boss had challenged him to improve the sales by ten percent, so I knew that George was looking for candy that flew off the shelves. I knew we had several products that would fulfill this challenge, so I asked George if he wanted a solution to the problem."

So at this point, Ron had successfully completed a number of the Steps of Sales.

1. **He felt good and ready to work because he had done his morning routine.**

2. **He was able to do some research about George and so by the time of the meeting he was well briefed on his background and his company. They shook hands when George arrived and got off to a great start.**

3. **George was confirmed as a qualified customer, with a problem to solve, plus the budget and authority to get it done.**

4. **The emotional trigger was the challenge from George's boss to improve candy sales by 10%.**

5. **Finally, Ron asked George for permission to proceed with the rest of the sales process.**

"Now I got to the heart of the meeting. Our company had a number of candy offerings that had proven track records of practically flying off the shelves. These candies practically sold themselves and I had the statistics to prove it.

I brought a large box to the meeting with a sample of each of our candies. One by one I pulled out each product and George and I discussed them briefly. I explained to George that these different candies worked together to sell each other. For example, we had learned through experience that three different kinds of chocolate would sell better if placed next to each other.

As I went through the presentation, I kept it interesting and on-point to George's emotional trigger and problem. I explained one benefit and got George to agree he wanted that for his chain of stores. I went on to talk about another one and got more agreement. I continued this over and over for about thirty minutes until we'd gone through the whole presentation. George was thrilled with the offering. We went through the rest of the sales steps, and by the end of the meeting he'd agreed to take on the entire selection for his stores."

This demonstrates step six of the sales process. In this step, you present your offer to the prospect. Up to this point, most of what you have been doing is listening to what the prospect has to say. You've asked questions and made some conclusions, but mostly you've been interested in getting information and approval to continue the process.

Keep in mind that this is not a technical presentation. You do not want to give a detailed explanation of how your product works or its internal structure.

Remember what you are selling—a solution to your prospect's problem that fulfills their emotional triggers. You are not selling based upon all the features of your product or service. If you focus on their problem and their triggers, you'll most likely get the sale. If you wander unnecessarily into the features they don't need you may find yourself with questions that you cannot answer. Plus, unless their emotional trigger *is* not the other features, you run the risk of not actually providing a solution to their problem

Your purpose in this step is to build a *yes pattern* and listen for buying signals with your prospect.

By the time you've gotten quite a few yes answers it's time to ask them for permission to move on to the next step.

Step 7:
Close on Product
Concepts

"There is no prize in sales for second place. It's win or nothing. The masters know this and strive for - they fight for - that winning edge."

–Jeffrey Gitomer

Have you ever presented the offer to the prospect only to be disappointed to find they really didn't want to make the purchase after all? It all felt so right and everything seemed to point to a successful sale, but your customer changed their mind and left empty-handed, leaving you with a mystery. What happened to the sale?

I'll tell you what happened. You probably forgot to close on product concepts. You never got your prospect's agreement that the solution you offered was something that was needed or wanted.

The IT director of a retail chain, Rich, related how he arranged a meeting with a salesperson, Kathy, to purchase almost a thousand computer systems. Kathy was new to the account, but had done her research, interviewing the previous salesperson by phone. She learned the history of the account, knew Rich was the decision maker, and had the money in his budget. She was also briefed on his emotional triggers.

Kathy felt the sales process with Rich went perfectly. He relaxed with her right away, and they quickly got down to business. Within an hour, Kathy had presented her solution, and she was sure that Rich was sold on the idea. She got so excited she told Rich the price and asked how he was going to pay.

She skipped step seven, Close on Product Concepts, and because of that she didn't get the sale. In fact, Rich was exasperated by the exchange. He was interested in their product, but felt it was not quite the right fit for his needs. Because Kathy didn't present the product concepts, he was not given the chance to agree or voice his objections to the solution offered. If Kathy had followed step seven, she would have known that he was not happy with her solution, and she could have taken a step back to re-explain and close on product concepts.

However, Kathy shouldn't feel too bad. Many salespeople skip this step because they think they have received agreement during the presentation or they just want to start asking for the money.

HOW TO CONFIRM THE PRODUCT CONCEPTS

The purpose of step seven is to get the prospect's agreement that the solution you presented in step six is both needed and wanted. If you remember, in previous steps you found out what problem needed to be solved and what emotional triggers needed to be fulfilled. At that point, you determined whether or not you had a product or service that addressed those needs. You then presented your solution to the prospect.

This is the point where many salespeople misunderstand the sales process. It's easy to make a mistake and believe the deal is already done. Prospects are often excited and interested during the presentation, especially if you present the offer correctly.

Don't make the mistake of believing that excitement is an agreement to continue with the sales process. Excitement and enthusiasm are important to making sales, but they are not an agreement.

Ask your prospect two questions.

1. **Based on everything we talked about, does the solution I presented sound like a winner?**

2. **Does it sound like the way you want to go?**

This is a very simple step. Don't overcomplicate it. You are asking your prospect if you've hit the bullseye with your proposed solution.

By asking these questions (or variations of them) you confirm that your prospect agrees with your solution and that you have approval to continue to the next step of the sales process.

If you have completed the previous steps correctly, then the answer to both questions should be an enthusiastic "yes." The steps before this point laid the groundwork and step seven is the clincher.

For example, your customer said he wanted a car because he needed transportation. He wants to impress the ladies (emotional trigger), so you presented a red convertible to him. It seemed like the perfect fit to resolve his problem and fulfill his emotional need.

But, when you asked if he agreed with the convertible, he said no, that it wasn't going to work. He loves the car, he explains, but he hates convertibles as they mess up his hair. Now you need to ensure that you have the problem fully understood before revisiting step four to further refine the emotional triggers.

Step seven is that simple. Before proceeding further into the sales process and closing the deal, you need to ensure that you actually have a solution that works for your customer. Once you've closed on product concepts, you can get your client's approval to continue with the sales process.

Let's go back to the example at the beginning of this chapter. If you recall, Kathy met with Rich, the IT director of a retail chain. Rich needed to purchase a thousand computers and had asked Kathy to come by and explain her solution.

Kathy worked through all of the steps. She knew he had a problem: Rich needed to replace all of the computers at each of the stores in the chain. She thought she understood his emotional triggers and believed that the performance of the system was most important to him. She did a wonderful presentation of her solution—a small, fast, nice-looking computer.

"So, Rich," Kathy began. "Based on everything we've discussed, does this solution work for you?"

Rich sat back in his chair and thought for a moment.

"You know, Kathy," he said. "No, it really doesn't do what I need."

Now Kathy has to ask a few questions to figure out what was missing from the proposal that she made. It didn't take long for her to find out he hadn't mentioned an important emotional trigger.

"Really?" Kathy asked. "Where does the proposal fall short?"

"Well," Rich said. "It's a great machine and I'm sure it would work great. But it's too small for our needs."

"Small?"

"Yes. The cabinet needs to be larger. You see, thieves can carry small computers out of the store too easily. We need the cabinets to be physically larger."

You see how cleanly Kathy jumped back to step four and identified another emotional trigger? The original computers she presented would have solved part of the problem nicely but didn't fulfill the additional criteria.

Fortunately, Kathy had a larger computer in her inventory, so she was able to complete the steps up through 6, fully this time, and then sailed right on through step seven, completed the remaining steps, and closed the deal.

Step 8: Close on Price and Terms

"If you really want to do something you will find a way, if not you will find an excuse."

–Jeff Rohn

At this point, I'll bet you think the deal is sealed. The work is done, and all that's left is to collect the money and deliver the product or service, right? It was a lot of effort to get here. The customer has agreed with everything you've put in front of them, so what else could be left to do?

Unfortunately, if you think the sale has been closed at this point, it's likely that you will be disappointed. The customer doesn't yet know the final price of the product or service and you have not discussed the terms and conditions of the sale.

Without getting an agreement on price and terms, the deal is not done, and it becomes very possible for the entire deal to unravel and disappear.

Let's look at an example. Ken is a car salesperson. One day, a young man, Ralph, came in and asked to look at cars. Ken helped Ralph select the perfect car, successfully worked him through all of the steps. He closed Ralph on step seven: Close on Product Concepts. Ralph loved the idea of a small, sporty car to impress his boss and the co-workers at his office. At this point, Ken was already thinking about his commission and how to spend the money and he forgot about step eight.

Instead of getting agreement on price and terms, Ken just said the car would cost $16,000 plus tax, and asked Ralph into his office to begin filling out the paperwork for financing.

Ralph was confused, since the price seemed a little high for that car, and he already had the financing lined up with his own bank. He was also a little bit annoyed because he was asked to pay without having agreed to a price yet.

CONFIRM THE PRICE AND TERMS

Have you noticed how much agreement comes up throughout this book? That's because getting your customer to agree, over and over, lowers their resistance, improves their trust in you (the salesperson), and creates excitement about the product or service you are offering.

They agree that they are the decision maker and have the money or budget for the sale; they agree that your product or service is a solution to their problem and fulfills their emotional needs; and finally, they concur that your solution is acceptable. This, in effect, is their approval to continue forward with the next rule.

By all means don't stop getting their agreement at this point. You've almost closed the deal and you have a chance of doing so if you just follow step eight: Close on Price and Terms.

This means that you need to tell the customer the price and payment terms and then get agreement that they are acceptable. This is also the point where you discuss things like warranties, service agreements, and delivery options.

You begin by letting your customer know the price of your product or service. Tell them the exact price they will be paying. Be sure to include taxes, fees, and any other hidden costs.

Discuss payment terms. Will they be paying by credit card or will the sale be financed? Can they use a purchase order, allowing thirty days for payment? The client may say, for example, that he doesn't have a credit card. This is tricky for many salespeople. Handle the objection by smoothly suggesting other forms of payment.

For instance, a friend of mine went into a furniture store to purchase a new couch. He spent over two hours with the sales representative, looking at dozens of pieces of furniture until he found precisely the correct item for his home. When the salesperson discussed price, my friend said he didn't have that much money available on his card. The salesperson said that was not a problem since they offered in-store credit. The objection was calmly and professionally handled and the sale was closed.

Other components of the sale, such as warranties, shipping, and service agreements, are discussed and agreed upon during this part of the sales process. Also, get agreement for any optional services that can be provided.

Immediately handle any objections as they come up. Be prepared for just about any kind of consideration. The customer may claim the price is too high, the warranty is insufficient, or even that he/she doesn't want to pay for shipping.

Some savvy customers may want to negotiate price and terms. Depending upon the policies and practices of your company, this is the time for those discussions to occur. It is important therefore for you to know how much room you have to negotiate on price and terms. Can you, if necessary, lower the price of the product or service? Are you able to add on the extended warranty for a lower cost? What options are available for shipping or delivery of the service?

Step 9:
Ask for Money

"The five most important things a salesperson
can do is 1) ask for the money, 2) ask for
the money, 3) ask for the money, 4) ask for
the money and 5) ask for the money."

– Cowboys Owner Jerry Jones

D o you know what presents the most difficulties
to salespeople? You might think it is making
the initial contact and establishing rapport
with people day in and day out. This can be a
challenge for some, but there is another area of the sales
process even more difficult to confront.

Talking to the client and discovering the problem they are
trying to solve is an area of improvement needed by many
salespeople. However, this is still not the area that is the
most difficult for them to handle.

The biggest challenge for the majority of salespeople is asking for the money.

The most important thing a salesman must do is get the money. The sale is not really closed until the cash is in hand. Up to this point your customer has been getting to know and trust you and you've been discussing the solution to his or her problem.

When you get to step nine, you've hit the make-or-break point for the sale. If you've done your job right, then getting the customer to pay or sign a contract should be simple. If you have been following the rules you learned in this book, and at our seminars, you've ensured that your prospect agrees at each step of the process.

It is the agreement that makes this process work so well. Your clients have agreed that they have a problem that needs to be solved, and they agreed with your solution to that problem. By this time, they have agreed not just to the solution, but to the price you've asked them to pay and terms of payment.

There isn't anything more they need to agree to and, assuming all the rules were done correctly, there shouldn't be any more discussion. All you need now is to finally close the deal.

For example, when you go into the car dealer to purchase a new automobile, you can see they usually have this portion of the sales process grooved in pretty well. You get to see the car, drive it around a bit, chat about the features, and finally head into the finance manager's department to work on the contract for financing. In this case, getting you to sign on the bottom line on the contract is a form of asking for the money.

Thus, you need to actually ask for the money. This can mean different things for different kinds of sales.

- **The simplest form is when the customer gives you cash, check, or a credit card on the spot. You just ask, "Which credit card would you like to use?" or something similar, and that's all there is to it.**

- **Sometimes getting the money means the customer signs a contract for goods or services legally binding the customer to agree to the terms of sale. In the case of an automobile, a finance agreement and other documents are signed, and when that's done you receive payment from the financial institution.**

- **For a consulting agreement, getting the money might mean receiving an initial down payment for the services.**

- **Often, asking for payment involves a purchase order being produced by the buyer.**

You've gone to a great deal of trouble during this process to gain your customer's respect, trust, and the sale. But what happens after the customer walks out of the door? What if the product is defective, the service technicians are lacking, or there is something they question about the product after they get it home?

You can lay the groundwork for future questions and any issues that might arise simply and easily by continuing to maintain the trust that you've worked so hard to earn.

If applicable, tell them about the warranty and their options should anything go wrong. Be sure to let them know if there are different options or an extended warranty as well. If the product is defective, your customer now knows he can get it replaced or repaired.

Talk to them about how the product will be shipped, and work with them for different alternatives, if applicable. They may want to use a different shipping company, for example, or they might want to save shipping charges and pick up the product themselves.

A friend of mine bought some furniture recently: a new couch and kitchen table. These are heavy items, and he didn't have access to a truck to pick up the products. He didn't have the money for the delivery charges, which amounted to another hundred dollars, and was ready to drop the sale even at that late stage.

The salesperson said he understood my friend's issues with getting the furniture home and worked out free shipping with his manager. The salesperson even made sure that the furniture was carted up the stairs to my friend's house and completely assembled. Sure, the furniture company had to pay for the shipping themselves, but they gained a customer for life. The next time my friend needs furniture he'll pick up the phone and call that salesperson.

This step doesn't end when the customer walks out the door or even receives the product or service. Depending upon the circumstances, you should plan to make a follow-up call or two back to the customer to make sure the product or service was delivered on time and in good condition. Your customer will appreciate your attention to detail.

Once you've got the money in hand or the contract has been signed, you have one more rule you need to complete before you can consider the sale successful.

Step 10:
Get Testimonials
and Referrals

*"In sales, a referral is the key to
the door of resistance."*

– Bo Bennett

At this point in the sales process, you may believe you are finished, as most salespeople do. You have the money (or a signed contract), and the customer has their product, so what could be left? If you've done everything right so far then they are happy with what they have received and you are feeling content with a job well done.

However, there remains one more step to complete: Get Testimonials and Referrals.

Let me relate a story about my days as a car salesman. Selling cars generally means you get to the dealership before it opens and stand around for the rest of the day, sometimes until closing, working on selling cars.

Every single day I got there early like everyone else and waited for the potential customers to arrive. Sometimes I stood around for hours until it was my turn to assist a prospect, and it literally took all day long just to sell a car or two. It was hard, exhausting work, especially on those days when I didn't close a sale at all.

I noticed another sales associate, Jim, who strolled in at 11 a.m. and left at 4 p.m. every single day. At first I thought he wasn't going to last very long because he never even tried to get customers off the street. How could he be selling cars if he wasn't on the floor? And how was he getting any sales at all considering that he worked in his office the entire time he was there?

One day a man came into our dealership and I walked over to him to start the sales process. But he insisted that he was there to talk to Jim, so I showed him the way to his office and went back to standing around waiting for people to come to me.

It was then that I noticed people coming in all day long just to see Jim. From my count, Jim was seeing more customers than the five of us out on the lot put together. Even more important was that he seemed to have a much higher closing rate than anyone else. I had to find out what was going on.

"Jim," I asked. "How come I never see you work the floor like the rest of us? What's going on?"

Jim sipped on his coffee and then said, "Well, I understand the power of the referrals and testimonials."

"Oh?"

"Yes," he answered with a smile. "The referral. You see, at the end of every sale, I ask each customer for at least three other people who might be interested in purchasing a car."

"They tell you that?"

"Oh, you bet," he replied.

"They refer a car salesman to their friends and family? Really?"

"They're happy to do it Ben; they're very happy with the whole process. They bought a car that served their needs, and I make sure they know that I am here for them if they have any issues or anything at all down the road."

"So you call them later to get your referrals?"

"Oh no! I get the referrals from my new customers before they even leave the shop."

"Why so fast?"

"Because at the close of the deal they are in a good place. They feel good about me, about the dealership, and about the purchase. It is the perfect time to ask them for the name of other friends or associates they would like to help. And they almost always provide me with those names in addition to writing a testimonial for me that other potential clients can read."

"What do you do with the referrals?"

"I give every single referral a call, of course. I tell them how I took care of their friend and that he or she was so happy with the service I provided that he/she gave me their name and number. I then invite them over for a free test drive and I'll even throw in a free coffee and donut. Of course they call their friend and ask him about me, and before you know it, another future client is walking in the door to make a purchase."

He took another sip of coffee as I took in this information.

"When the prospect calls me back, I schedule an appointment so I don't have to wait here all day. The reason why I work half the time as everyone else is because I don't work on walk-ins; I work on getting qualified appointments and the testimonials posted online help bring in other future clients."

"Qualified appointments that you get through referrals."

"Exactly! I get the clients to come to me. Better still, they are halfway sold already, simply because their friends or associates recommended me to them. A lot of the work has already been done and all I need to do is complete the deal."

Do you see how that works? You ask for referrals right after the sale has closed and the customer has paid. Generally, at this point they are feeling pretty good about the whole thing and will happily give you some referrals.

You've talked with your clients, gained their confidence and trust, and created a yes pattern that's hard to resist. On top of that, they have agreed with everything to get to this point. You gave them not just a solution to their problem, but you fulfilled their emotional need as well.

They are probably never going to feel better than this about the sale, you, your product or service, and your company.

That's the right time to ask them for a little something in return.

Don't wait; a better time will not present itself. Get those referrals.

Make sure they know you are looking for people who might want your product or service. Random phone calls to uninterested people don't do much good. For example, if you are selling smart phones, ask your customer who else might benefit from a new smart phone. This way your client is giving your pre-qualified leads and those are extremely valuable.

Be sure, while you are at it, to ask them to write a testimonial. Many customers will be happy to spend a few minutes writing down how wonderful the sale went, how great you were as a salesperson, or how fantastic they feel now that they have the product. You can use these testimonials in your marketing and advertising, which in turn brings even more customers in the door.

Start making some phone calls once you have your list of referrals. Be sure to mention who gave you their name. This will help smooth the way since a trusted person recommended you.

With the referral ball rolling, you will have pre-qualified customers flocking to your door. That's a lot easier than pounding the pavement and looking for someone to purchase your product or service.

Conclusion

Regardless of the type of business you are in, to be successful you need to be thoroughly trained. Remember, a key component of all business is sales. In fact, no matter what you do in life, sales is involved in some way. Whether you run a company, are in sales, or you manage salespeople, you need to invest in the training to help you and your team improve the bottom line.

Here at 360 Sales Consulting we provide training for a sales process that you can use every day to close more sales, make customers happier, and bring in more income.

Wouldn't you like to increase your income while decreasing the amount of work and frustration involved in selling? Would you like to spend your time at work being more productive? Would you enjoy improving your relationship with your customers?

Visit our web site today: www.360SalesConsulting.com

Bonus Offers:

Three FREE sales training videos

Daily planner to keep you on track every day!

Download them here:
www.360SalesConsulting.com

Acknowledgements

Many people helped me get to where I am today. The list of those to whom I am grateful is very long and could require a book all on its own.

I'd like to begin by thanking my wife for her support and for the love and encouragement that she has shown me throughout our relationship. Without her backing, I do not believe I would be as successful as I am today.

I am especially grateful to my father for his stern discipline, which is what it takes to succeed in sales. The support of my family has always been there, and I have learned so much from them about friendship, love, and support. My mother, who has since passed away, inspired me to go for my dreams.

The United States Marines also deserve lots of credit for teaching me how to stay motivated, focused, and determined; skills you need to write and finish a book!

Joe Yazbeck is my public speaking coach and motivated me to write this book. With his friendship and advice, he has pointed me in the direction of helping people and gaining success.

JV Crumb III was my mentor for many years, and I would not be here today without his knowledge, experience, and willingness to share what he knew with me.

The experiences of working with Stewart Vespee, the man who taught me sales, were invaluable in shaping my career and life. When I started in the gym business, he taught me how to sell and recruited me into the sales department.

I owe special thanks to Eli Gonzalez of The Ghost Publishing, and Richard Lowe Jr. Their help in putting this book together was invaluable.

A big thank you also goes to book cover designer: Margie Rosenstein of NuEdgePhotoDesign.com

Finally, I would like to thank Howard VanEs and his team at Let's Write Books, Inc. who packaged up this book and took it through the publishing process.

Recommended Reading

Little Red Book of Sales
    By Jeffrey Gitomer

    This book aims to bring understanding of why people
    buy, which is, according to the author, "all that
    matters."

Think and Grow Rich
    By Napoleon Hill

    This was the first book to question, "What makes a
    winner?" It is the ultimate motivational book. The
    author draws on stories of millionaires such as
    Andrew Carnegie, Thomas Edison, and Henry Ford to
    illustrate the principles he describes.

The E-myth Revised
    By Michael E. Gerber

    This classic dispels all of the myths related to starting
    your own business. The author points out the things
    that can get in the way of starting a successful

business. He breaks down all of the stages of the life of a business and gives the reader the information needed to successfully run their own company.

No Fear Speaking
By Joe Yazbeck

Longtime master coach, performer, and founder of the No Fear Speaking System, Joe Yazbeck, will show you step-by-step how to create and deliver powerful presentations, master the artful science of public speaking, and deliver impact speeches and presentations.

About the Author

Benjamin Brown is CEO of 360 Sales Consulting, a company specializing in helping businesses and entrepreneurs excel in sales and dramatically increase their bottom line. Their proprietary sales system has become recognized as a "game changer" and is in demand by companies of all sizes throughout the United States.

Ben's sales career of more than twenty years began with selling health club memberships and quickly worked into sales manager and sales director positions. Ben's diverse experience includes selling vehicles, computer products and services, voice recognition software, staffing services, and transportation services.

Due to his success, Ben soon became in demand for sales training, which led him to create the 10-step sales process detailed in this book.

Ben is a former United States Marine with six years of service and a veteran of the Gulf War. He currently resides with his wife and family in the Tampa Bay Florida area.

Notes:

Notes:

Notes:

Notes: